T0380680

Hello Beautiful

LAURA VEMA BELL

BALBOA.PRESS

A DIVISION OF HAY HOUSE

Balboa Press books may be ordered through booksellers or by contacting:

Balboa Press
A Division of Hay House
1663 Liberty Drive
Bloomington, IN 47403
www.balboapress.com
844-682-1282

Print information available on the last page.

ISBN: 979-8-7652-5057-0 (sc)
ISBN: 979-8-7652-5058-7 (e)

Library of Congress Control Number: 2024905967

Balboa Press rev. date: 06/10/2024

Contents

Dedication

I dedicate this book to my mother, who just turned ninety-six in February 2023. She grew up picking cotton and worked hard raising five children. I also dedicate it to the beautiful women in my life who support me each day by loving and accepting me just the way I am. I am. Special thanks to my sister, my daughter, my three daughters-in-law, and my two granddaughters. So many women have touched my heart in many ways, and you know who you are. Thank you so much for your love, truth, and support. This is for you beautiful ladies!

Introduction

This journal has been written with love, courage, vulnerability, humor, and a lot of life experiences. Each section is written with a lesson I have learned about myself and others and experiences I've had over my lifetime. I hope that my stories and questions will resonate with you, and you will have your own discoveries as you answer the questions I have asked. The subjects, I hope, will move and inspire you to pull back the curtain so you will grow emotionally and spiritually, discover parts of yourself, and reveal your true inner beauty.

Many times, in my life, when I was ready, the teacher appeared. I hope this book will be your teacher in some way. While you may not read or may not feel a need to complete each section, I hope you will find something here that will help you in some way. Most of all, I hope that you will feel the love and connection I am sending to you. It says that no matter what your life has given you so far, you are beautiful right now in this moment. If you are not where you want to be or not feeling how you want to feel, you have choices. You can change your life and you can be happy. You have the power within you. Life is an adventure and one of continuous growth if you are open to it. Don't let fear hold you back. I have always told my children there is a fine line between fear and excitement, and it's how you look at it.

You can complete this book in your own time, in your own way. It may be beneficial to complete it with other women or a woman you trust and who knows you well. There are many benefits of an intimate conversation and revealing yourself openly to a non-judgmental friend. This friend will share her experience and feelings with you and express what she sees in you. That is how intimacy is formed and love is received and given. And so, we begin.

Preface

The year was 1960. It was a dark and lonely night on a dirt road a mile from the nearest neighbor. There, a little ten-year-old girl prayed to God that, if he brought her mom and dad safely home to her, she promised to grow up and do something in her life that would help make other people's lives better. Well, they did come home, and that loving child grew up and carried love in her heart for everyone to the best of her ability. That child was me; I really did try to walk with love in my heart for everyone most of my life. I felt that to be connected to God (or another entity or nothing at all, depending on preference), that spirit needed to be in my life to bring me true happiness, which is love and acceptance of myself and others. I have often described my purpose in life as "love." I know you may think that it is an easy purpose, and I don't have to do much. It doesn't cost a lot of money or time to do it. I challenge you to try and let me know how you do. If I hadn't mentioned it, I wrote this book to challenge you with humor. I feel that life is so much easier with humor and laughter.

My home life as a child was one of poverty, financial and emotional. My dad was a lobsterman in the summer and logger in the woods in the winter. We grew up with a back house and no running water except for a pump at the sink. This made washing clothes in the wringer washer a bit easier than with the scrub board, which my mom used when we arrived at the old cape farmhouse. At one point, we had nine people in our farmhouse: five children and four adults. We finally moved when I was eleven. After we moved, we could see Christmas lights and go to movies. We were all excited. At that point, Mom and Dad divorced. Things became tougher for my mom, who was taking care of five children by herself. This was 1961 when there was no state aid and no assistance for families other than from city offices or churches. Thank goodness today we have so many resources available for mothers and children, and opportunities for women to receive childcare so they are able to work.

My twenties were busy years. I struggled with showing and receiving love. By the time I was thirty-two, I had married three times. I started counseling and groups at twenty-nine and continued for years, hoping it would give me peace, happiness, and a sense of being good enough. My third and final marriage, when I was thirty-two, lasted for thirty-one years, until my husband Michael passed away in 2013. After ten years of marriage to Michael, I finally realized that my happiness wasn't someone else's responsibility. Finding someone else to make me happy was not going to happen. I had found a man who would do anything for me and give me anything I wanted, but still I was not happy. It was time to look at why I wasn't happy. I recognized I was holding myself back from true happiness. Fear, insecurity, and unhappiness were controlling my life. The conversations in my head were there to distract me. They continued to keep me from the source of my power and my true soul's essence of love for myself and others.

Not conscious of the promise I made as I went through my life, I'd like to believe I still made more loving and kind gestures toward people than mean and hurtful things. The universe decided to remind me of my promise and give me a way to deliver love and kindness. It sent two different psychics along my travels in the last seven years. I had the opportunity to wander into a psychic's home in Savannah, Georgia. She told me I would be writing a book; I quickly told her she was not talking to the right girl. She said I was going to write a book and she saw me signing copies.

I thought about it and said, "Well, I have always wanted to work with teenage girls about self-esteem."

"Nope, you're signing books for older women." I dismissed the whole idea because, clearly, I couldn't write a book. My writing experience was very limited, and I was no expert on self-esteem. Fast forward six years and another spiritual medium said the same thing. I told both that I could barely talk let alone write a book. Yet, here I am writing a book. I won't be winning any awards, but I am going to trust and believe that the lessons I have learned will be of some type of guidance to you. If you come away feeling more empowered in your life after reading this book, I will be blessed as well.

This book would not have been written in a million years if not for all the women in my life who were there to be a reflection in which to see myself. They were my mirror to see myself, the good, the bad, and the ugly. These women have been there and stood by me many times throughout the last thirty and more years. Others were there before, but I didn't trust them because I didn't I trust myself. I thank them for sticking with me.

Many different avenues for developing self-esteem are on the market that you could read or listen to. I created this book so when you finish, you will have discovered something within yourself you can use as you journey through life. I hope it will help you be true to yourself and bring out parts of yourself that support living in your highest self, full of self-love and love for others. Be yourself at the highest level. Now, let's discover the parts of yourself that you may not be in touch with, that you will fall in love with, and that you will be proud to show others. Soon, everyone will be saying, "Hello beautiful."

Knowing Yourself

S O MANY WOMEN IN MY LIFE HAVE BEEN INSTRUMENTAL IN MY SUCCESSES. SOME women, whose names I cannot remember, will never be forgotten. I will begin in 1979. I was twenty-nine years old, living in a three-bedroom trailer with my son and daughter. I was working forty hours a week with my ex-husband, "together" for the third time. Yes, I said the third time—I don't give up easily. I thought if I loved him enough, we could overcome anything. I had no financial support or working car and felt trapped. I began riding with a coworker, who was just finishing college at the age of fifty-two. She convinced me that I could handle going to college and continue working. My experience with education has not been very good. I dropped out of high school twice and finally returned to earn my GED four years after my class graduated. I continued classes at a local business school. Being hopeful, I took a leap of faith and enrolled in a local university. In my psychology class, my teacher was discussing addictions and related her personal experiences with Al-Anon family groups. Her conversation and her vulnerability gave me hope and encouragement. I immediately contacted her and made an appointment to speak with her outside of class. I am forever grateful for her courage in sharing her story with us. It gave me hope that I could have peace and a loving home for my children. This was the beginning of learning about myself as a co-dependent mate and daughter of an alcoholic.

I learned how to use tools to separate myself from my ex-husband, both physically and mentally. I began believing in myself and my own self-worth. For the first time in my life, I wrote goals for myself. Nadine taught me to believe in myself, and know that I had the power to change my life and stop being a victim. What I learned in Al-Anon was that I was not alone, and I had a voice. I didn't like that I couldn't make everything about the alcoholic. I had to focus on what I was responsible for and find the courage to change myself. Al-Anon offers so many useful tools to apply in your life to become independent. All my relationships changed from this one action.

Once I realized I had the power to make changes and I was no longer a victim of my own beliefs, I was a sponge. I continued to look for ways to better myself, to take responsibility for my family's future, and to be a better mother and human being. I was always asking myself questions to find out what I really wanted. I no longer lived under others' expectations of me. I learned to love. I embraced the questions and was not afraid of the answers. It is so easy to go through life with one day leading to the next day, one week leading to the next week, and one year leading to the next year. Before you know it, your life is nearing the end.

To know and accept all of yourself is where true freedom lives. To love yourself and others and be open to having true joy in your life is freedom. This one action of trusting another woman who cared for me led me to believe in myself and recognize my true value. I wanted to continue a lifetime of discovering all the universe would lead me toward. While I never finished my college education, I continued to put continuing education as a part of my life.

I learned I wasn't stuck in the life I was living. I had choices. I believed in myself. I could do it if I tried, and not to be afraid of failing. I wanted to give my children a better life. I needed to be responsible for my own happiness by going back to school and changing my environment.

What do you know about yourself to be true?

_____

_____

_____

_____

_____

_____

_____

_____

_____

_____

_____

_____

_____

What do you need to do to be responsible for your happiness?

_____

_____

_____

_____

_____

_____

_____

_____

_____

_____

_____

_____

_____

_____

All of Me

*I*T IS SO EASY TO ADMIT WHAT WE LOVE ABOUT OURSELVES AND THE CHARACTERISTICS that describe our greatest qualities. However, it's difficult to admit what we don't like about ourselves. Let's take the time to go on a little discovery trip into our souls and our minds and be honest with ourselves. When we are honest with ourselves about all the feelings and thoughts we have, then we can truly accept them. This is when we feel true love for ourselves. When we judge those characteristics and feelings as unacceptable, we are not able to fully love ourselves.

For seventeen years, I belonged to a women's group of several different kinds. In one, we discussed the subject of how judgmental we could be sometimes. However, I had difficulty even admitting that I judged anyone—to the point I was a bit slimy. My ego told me my judgments were only made to compare myself to others, and I had to judge them to judge myself. Yep, Miss Goody Two Shoes. Because I had made a promise to live up to an image of love and kindness, I wasn't going to admit I was judgmental. I certainly was not going to admit all of my other unbecoming characteristics. It took openness, honesty, and awareness to admit my shortcomings. Even my good behavior at that time was not anything I could readily admit to others or myself—that would be boastful and vain. I had not loved myself enough to even admit my good qualities, let alone accept that someone else recognized them in me.

Other women gave me the courage to look at myself openly with no judgments. I was with like-minded women who were willing to express themselves fully and honestly, with a little bit of struggle. I felt so much freedom in seeing them reflected in me, so much freedom in accepting myself and accepting them. Our freedom sets us free to be real. It is as if you stripped naked for all to see your imperfections while still loving every bit of yourself. Maybe that's why there are so many strippers.

After quite a bit of soul-searching, I discovered I am kind, spiritual, strong, and passionate. I can be bitchy, opinionated, stubborn, and untruthful. I am also vulnerable, brave, and intuitive. At times, I am catty, hateful, mean, and feel like a victim. Finally, I am trustworthy, forgiving, loyal, hopeful, funny, thoughtful, loving, kind, and spirited.

You may want to do this activity with women you trust. The truth for me is I was ready to pull off the layers covering my true self, and I was able to discover the essence of my soul, which I may never have known. Sometimes we can't see all of the characteristics that we possess or believe in ourselves. A friend will tell you what she sees. These parts of me were never revealed as a child because of fear and lack of knowledge. That inner child spirit was never able to show itself. Do not fear; there is no deadline to stop you from letting your free spirit and inner child out. You don't know what you don't know until you have a willingness to go digging for the answers. You may think they are skeletons but really, they are the treasures you have been looking for.

Other women will show you who you are, so seek out like-minded women. They are our mirrors who reflect to us ourselves. You will see the good, the bad, and the ugly, so you will love and accept all of yourself and can shine as the beautiful spirit you are. I sat and took it all in. By listening, I found myself. When another person shared, I heard myself and understood why I felt the way I did; we had the same experience. I had long forgotten the experience or was unaware of what it meant to me.

I am very grateful for their awareness, openness, and vulnerability. I learned that by revealing myself and accepting both the bad and the good, I could love all of myself. I stopped trying to be anything except who I was at any given moment. I did not have to change one thing about myself to love myself or work hard to be perfect for someone else to love me. What a gift to me!

What are the behaviors I don't like about myself and/or want others to see?

_____

_____

_____

_____

_____

_____

_____

_____

_____

_____

_____

_____

_____

_____

What are the behaviors I love about myself?

_____

_____

_____

_____

_____

_____

_____

_____

_____

_____

_____

_____

_____

_____

Low Self-Esteem

WHEN I HAVE LOW SELF-ESTEEM AND I DO NOT LOVE MYSELF, LIFE IS HARD. I don't believe in myself. I don't believe that anything can be changed. I feel hopeless, I am easily angered, and everything (seriously, everything) is a problem. I am awake for hours at night with anxiety, worrying about the future or what I did wrong in the past. I think that I shouldn't be myself, I have no choice, and I feel lonely. There is a big pity party going on inside for sure. Sometimes, I can see what the trigger was that dropped me into what I call the dark side. Sometimes, it is not obvious to me until I look around and I am making everyone wrong in some way because of it. I have not been living with integrity and addressing the problems as they come up. I become overwhelmed by life. I see myself running around, avoiding issues, until I make a big circle and smack my head on this big wall I have created. Quite often I am forced to stop by my own body when it says, "Hold on there for one minute. You have not given me any love. You run around and do not rest. You try to avoid your problems. Now I'm sick, and you are going to stop whether you want to or not." I end up down and out with vertigo, unable to get up. Most of all, I don't like myself, much less love myself. I will say that it only happens once or twice a year. My own unrealistic expectations cause most of my low self-esteem. Wanting to be better and do more but not caring for myself physically are surefire ways to end up drained and in low spirits.

These are a few of my triggers and signs of my low self-esteem and depression.

- I think I have no choices.
- I do not take care of myself or get enough rest.
- I think of myself as a victim and do not take responsibility.
- I allow myself to be surrounded by negativity.
- I have unrealistic expectations of myself and others.
- I have to control and know what is going to happen.
- I judge others and myself.

If you have low self-esteem, what are some of the signs and triggers, and when do these happen?

_____

_____

_____

_____

_____

_____

_____

_____

_____

_____

_____

_____

_____

High Self-Esteem

MY DEFINITION OF SELF-ESTEEM IS SELF-LOVE. WHEN MY SELF-ESTEEM IS high, I live in love and am at my very best as a human being. When I do not love myself, I am not a loving, spiritual being and I do not like myself.

When I feel good about myself, I am open to the outside world and display loving energy around me. The characteristics of my self-esteem are joy, openness to others, and trust that I can handle whatever happens. I'm aware of others and accept their opinions. I am a better listener. I laugh more and can laugh at myself. I don't take things others say personally. I dance anywhere and anytime I want. I love to dance; I feel the music rather than just hear it, so I must move my body. I am more playful and not ashamed or embarrassed to be childlike. I feel young and feel like life has so much more to teach me.

One of the ways I regain high self-esteem is by talking with a friend who will listen and not try to change how I am feeling. She will listen to me and acknowledge what I am saying. When I can vent to someone who does not judge me and recognizes my humanity, I feel good about myself for my creativity. I really appreciate it. I fall back to YouTube and look for ways to improve myself and/or ways to understand what I am going through. I take a bath and pamper myself or go outside to be closer to nature. Those things always help me feel better. Depending on whether I have made myself physically sick or am well, I will get up and make myself do something, take some kind of action. I will go out and connect with people, I listen to music and dance in my kitchen, or I will do something for someone else.

These are signs my life is going well and I am loving myself.

- My spirit and health are purring like a kitten.
- I have no problems, just challenges.
- I can see my choices clearly.

- I trust in the universe; I believe everything will work out.
- Everything seems easy.
- I am in love with myself and others.
- I am excited about life and the opportunities.
- I have a positive attitude and I am happy.

What are some of your behaviors and signs that your life is working and you are living in high self-esteem?

_____

_____

_____

_____

_____

_____

_____

_____

_____

_____

_____

_____

_____

_____

You Are Not Your Ego

W HEN MY TEN-YEAR-OLD SELF SPOKE TOTALLY FROM INNOCENCE AND TRUST in God, it was purely from my soul. We are all born innocent and pure. Our egos develop as we develop our selves individually. We are unique because of our experiences. Much of what we do and think is controlled by our egos and unconnected to our true selves, our souls, or intuition.

Our egos are there to protect us from outside influences and tell us we are special and unique. They distinguish us from others. They can tell us we are amazing and support us in achieving our dreams come true. They tell us we are good enough. They gather all of the information for our lives and save it for when it's needed to protect us or drive us forward. If we do not behave the way they think we should, they tell us we are stupid and not good enough compared to others. They question our motives, asking, "Why are you doing that?" and "Why can't you do better?" They remember every time our parents said, "You are stupid" and the kids we played with said, "You're ugly. You can't play with us." Whatever they hear, they store.

If you are unfortunate not to have had the love and care you deserved as a child, you are limited to the care of your ego. It covers up the unfed soul and takes control. For those of us who never developed empathy and compassion from our parents or another loving adult, egos can be disastrous. They can lead us into narcissism or other behavioral problems.

Most of us have had someone along the way to adulthood tell us we are not good enough. With today's media and our exposure to so many other people's opinions, questioning our self-worth and values is almost unavoidable,

My story was I was stupid. I didn't know it then, but I am dyslexic and have attention deficit disorder (ADD). I was never professionally diagnosed. I decided at one point in my life that

I am what I am, and I like myself just fine. I only bring up the stupid story so it may help you realize yours and kick your story to the curb. Find ways to connect with your heart and soul. The sooner you learn this, the sooner you will find happiness.

Please take your time thinking about all the messages that you have heard and believed. Choose one that convinced you are less than a beautiful and soulful self. I know it may be scary to dig up the past, but it will be worth it when you find the story that repeats itself and says you are not good enough. Once you find it, you are going to read it out loud to yourself or someone else. Then, you are going to burn it. That story is not part of who you are so rid yourself of it.

Celebrate it being gone and write a new story to replace it. The story I replaced mine with is "I am bright and intelligent and can do anything I want."

Listen to what is being said about you. What is the conversation you hear and what are you thinking about yourself? Most of the time, we are not even aware of the conversations being spoken in our minds. Whatever you find to be yours, replace it with what is true and create your *new story.*

Do you know what your ego tells you (your story) repeatedly that is not true?

_____

_____

_____

_____

_____

_____

_____

_____

_____

_____

_____

_____

_____

What is your new story?

_____

_____

_____

_____

_____

_____

_____

_____

_____

_____

_____

_____

_____

Your Ego and Relationships

WHEN I STARTED LIVING CONSCIOUSLY, DELIBERATELY AND WITH CLEAR intention, I became more aware of what triggered me. I realized I could choose how to respond. I became more responsible for my relationships. I paid more attention to the conversations in my head that were from my ego and those from my heart and soul. I learned when I was responding from my true self or from my ego. I often asked myself, "Who is speaking for me: my spirit or my ego? Why is my ego present? What am I afraid of or challenged by?"

The ego I refer to is so strong it keeps you separate and unable to empathize and connect with others in a loving, positive way. I would encourage everyone to have a healthy ego and celebrate his or her individuality. When my ego feels threatened by someone or something, it becomes very unfriendly and protective. I'm going to name my ego to differentiate between my ego and my heart and soul. "Zap" is like a bolt of lightning that comes out of nowhere, and I can feel it building up. When Zap hits a blow, I know it. Most of the time, I am not even aware it's heating up and it just hangs around interfering with my relationships inside and outside of myself. Don't get me wrong. Zap can help me overcome my fears and remind me of how strong and worthy I am of anything I choose to be or do. However, Zap can be a bit overprotective and overbearing as well. I don't want my ego, good old Zap, to keep me from having close, trusting, and intimate relationships. Knowing when Zap is around and not being useful is not always easy. However, I can identify when Zap is showing up if I am living in the present and living consciously.

What are the signs that my ego Zap is present?

- I speak and say things I wouldn't normally say, such as swear words.
- I become angry but do not say anything and carry the resentment inside.
- I gossip about what happened rather than speak with the person.

- Everything is a problem; my thinking is negative, stinking thinking.
- I don't see that I have choices.
- I take everything personally, as if everything said is meant to be about me.
- I don't accept another person's opinion and thoughts and believe that mine is the only the right one.
- I am judgmental of myself and others.
- I have expectations of others.
- I am stupidly brave and throw caution to the wind.
- I try to convince others I know more than I do; I make up stuff to be right.

Are you aware of when your ego is present and when it isn't? What would you name your ego?

_____

_____

_____

_____

_____

_____

_____

_____

_____

_____

_____

_____

_____

I have never named my healthy spirit or healthy ego. I know it's only one ego, and if I had two, they would be fighting, I'm sure. There would be Zap and Zippy that is peaceful, loving, fun, confident, and strong. When I was growing up, a woman who had a big ego or shared her successes it was not considered a good thing. She was not encouraged to show off or be proud of her accomplishments. That was not the norm for women. If you had a big ego, you couldn't be loving and kind or feminine and were thought of as masculine. If we had egos and were proud, that would be considered bragging and unladylike. Well, I am proud and not ashamed to say so. I'm going to call my ego Zippy when it's good and showing up as high spirited. I am reminded of a cartoon character with a good angel on one shoulder and the devil on the other, Zap and Zippy.

These are some ways I know Zippy is present.

- I am proud of something I have said and done and want to share my success with others. If bragging is what you want to call it, that is okay. It is okay to let yourself shine. Your happiness will be contiguous.
- Zippy is a direct reflection of my true spirit and I behave more in line with my heart.
- I am joyful and grateful.
- I don't fear the unknown
- I am brave.
- I am more caring toward others.
- I am outgoing.
- I am more connected to nature and other people.
- I am peaceful and full of hope.
- There are no problems that can't be solved.
- I balance health, family, and work, and live by my priorities.
- I trust in the universe and know that all will be okay.
- I can manifest what I want.

Have fun with this. Talk to someone you trust and who knows you. Be open and honest about what you are learning about yourself.

When does your ego (higher self) show up and shine?

_____

_____

_____

_____

_____

_____

_____

_____

_____

_____

_____

_____

_____

_____

_____

Being

I HAD THE OPPORTUNITY TO HEAR MAYA ANGELOU SPEAK A FEW YEARS BEFORE SHE passed, and I was in awe of her vulnerability and honesty. She was so present to everyone in the room, and you felt her energy and love for the thousands there. We never know how what we say or do to or for someone else will affect them. To us it does not seem that important, but to them they may be huge. Women come up to me who I haven't seen in years and say that I saved their marriages or that some statement I made to them changed their lives. They have shared it with others because it made them aware of something that changed them or their families for the better.

Never underestimate your value to another person. The smallest of actions or statements may be miracles to them. Have you ever been having a crazy day when one more thing would cause you to explode, but someone with a big smile held the door open, looked you in the eye, and said, "Have a wonderful day." That probably changed your feelings. Maybe a person subjected you to his or her angry feelings and it felt like you took on all those bad feelings by the time you left the room. We can be easily connected to others energetically and be unaware of it. Being conscious of my energy and what I put out into the world has been a continuing process all my life. Even as a child, I had an awareness and felt it was important to display kindness and be careful with my words. When we become aware of our ability to connect to our higher selves and put that energy out into the world, we make a difference in everything we do because we are being our true selves. A phrase that my daughter-in-law, Leslie, says frequently is "You be you." What a great statement about being yourself and encouraging and allowing people to just *be*.

In my early fifties, I was diagnosed with rheumatoid arthritis. At that time, it was debilitating. I was having issues with all my joints and was unable to do normal everyday things. My grandfather Erland passed away at age sixty-one when I was fifteen. I was very frightened that my future would be as painful and limited as his.

My whole life has involved loving and taking care of others. I was having a hard time wrapping my mind around what I would I do if I couldn't continue. What value would I be to anyone? I went into quite the pity party for sure. I had I heard about a women's weekend in Massachusetts. I would recommend it for every woman who has a desire to improve and discover more about herself. I found it very spiritual as well. I went, wanting to have peace with this major change in my life. I wanted to find acceptance of my disease and to be in touch with the loss of my mother-in-law Francis, who had just passed away a few months before in 2001. I was full of hope and open to discovering what was there for me. These experiences were always a bit frightening, but I was confident that I would discover something about myself and become a better version of myself.

I was given a room with a beautiful woman about ten years younger than me. She had muscular dystrophy and was confined to a wheelchair. I was not really surprised to find her there because the universe gives you what you need when you are ready. After meeting her and spending a few days with her, I found there was no room to feel sorry or that she was less of a person. She had the love of her life, two great children, and was vibrant, spirited, confident, and full of love. The way she would *be* was peaceful and gentle, inviting and confident. She was unafraid to ask for help and showed no shame or embarrassment, which I was really struggling with. To me, it was almost impossible to ask for help because of my fear of rejection and vulnerability. I thought that I was weak and needy. She gave me a huge gift by just being herself. Her value to me was priceless; her strength and acceptance were admirable. I really appreciate the memory of her and the value she brings in this moment as well. I hope wherever she is, she feels the energy and love I am sending her way. My willingness to ask her for help and "be" open and unafraid, and her vulnerability, honesty, and realness taught me that you do not give up anything that really matters when you are "being" authentic and living from love and spirit.

If we have the consciousness to be present in every moment we are in and live our authentic selves to those who are present to us, our lives will change and so will theirs. The smallest actions can make a difference in the energy of the world if we are all living with kindness, compassion, and forgiveness for ourselves and others. Let us start with ourselves and *be* our very best.

What does it mean to *just be* with someone? For me, it means being present, paying attention, listening with no interruptions, not processing my own thoughts about what they said, not responding, and connecting spiritually. Not all conversations are give and take. Sometimes, you just need to be present and a good listener. Either way, your presence requires you to be there in the essence of who you are.

My way of being is this: I am living in the moment, and I choose to be an example of love and acceptance. I am vulnerable and willing to be honest with others. I am unafraid to be my authentic self. I *be* love.

What energy do you put into the world? How do you *be*?

_____

_____

_____

_____

_____

_____

_____

_____

_____

_____

_____

_____

_____

_____

What do you want others to feel from you that you are not presently *being*?

_____

_____

_____

_____

_____

_____

_____

_____

_____

_____

_____

_____

_____

Choices

HOW MANY OF YOU HAVE STRUGGLED WITH CHOICES IN YOUR LIVES? MOST of us have, I'm sure. As busy people and with so many choices, our time becomes more limited. If you are like me, you want it all. Not all my choices are about things I like to do. They can be the demands of those around me, which are more like requirements than choices. Sometimes I must choose between more than one thing that means a lot to me, and it is difficult to choose which one. For some people, making choices is not easy at all. I happen to be one of those people who has no problems making choices and I usually know what I want immediately. I am a bit fearless and trust in the universe and spirit holding and understanding what I want to happen. When it gets difficult for me, I must choose between two equally important events or people. Knowing my priorities makes a difference.

An example could be choosing between my son's dirt bike race or my company's semi-annual awards luncheon.

How do you choose? This is a tough decision. I chose my son's race because he is my priority over my job. I learned that putting your life in the order of your priorities and living by those priorities makes choices so much easier. Until I realized what my priorities were, I was having difficulty because I did not want to disappoint anyone. I would torture myself while deciding. By making a list of the top three things in my life, what was important to me became simple.

Mine is:

1. My health and spirituality
2. Family
3. Work

I'm not saying that my list is perfect, but it is really what I am going to focus on today and in the future. Most of my life I have made family, friends, and work come before myself and my spiritual beliefs. This is when you will hear me say, "Take my advice. I'm not using it." I have decided to write them down as my priorities and see how It works. My childhood message was work first then play. That is fine if, as a child, you had two or three chores. When you are an adult with a world of responsibilities, you can become lost and resentful, even when you are making the choices.

In what order would you put your priorities and why?

1. _____

2. _____

3. _____

This next section is about decisions that you are having a hard time making. Not all choices can be made by making a list of the pros and cons, which is a very good idea in any choice. I learned this technique and found it can be very effective in helping me realize what those choices would feel like to me. You need to be in a quiet space and perhaps by yourself; this is not necessary if the other person is silent.

1. Find a very comfortable chair or sofa to sit on.
2. Close your eyes.
3. Take three or four deep breaths and relax.
4. Think of one of your choices and imagine what it would be like if you made that choice. Sit in that experience for a few minutes. What does it feel like? Picture yourself in the experience. When you feel like you have connected with the feelings it would evoke, bring yourself back to reality.
5. Think of what the other choice is and imagine yourself in that place or choosing that item. Put it on, wear it, smell it, and so on, and see yourself doing it. What does it feel like? Come back to reality.

6. Take a few minutes to analyze and decide which one was more comfortable, brought you more joy, or felt like the best choice.

At first, this may seem like a silly way to decide, but you will find it easier to do as you become more in touch with your intuition. Our intuition is there guiding us all the time. Listen to what is being stated in your mind that you weren't expecting.

Are there two choices you are struggling with that you could use with this procedure? Write down what you heard yourself saying and what you felt for each choice.

_____

_____

_____

_____

_____

_____

_____

_____

_____

_____

_____

_____

_____

What Kind of Man

THIS COULD BE A VERY LENGTHY SUBJECT FOR ME BECAUSE I AM STILL LEARNING every day about myself and my relationships with men. Even at the age of seventy-two, I keep on learning, thank goodness. Some of us look for challenges and, for some of us, challenges are dropped in our laps by the universe. Being brought up in a home with three brothers, one would assume I would know everything at an early age that I would need to know for the rest of my life. We were free-range children. I certainly learned to stand my ground and bring all I had when protecting myself. As you might think, we were a bit unruly. After all, we grew up when the Three Stooges was all there was. My two older brothers practiced on me when they got tired of each other. Just picture two children being held back by their collars, and you will have a good picture of what it was like. We were five children on a farm, free to roam and live adventurously. I am now a proud grandmother to seven wonderful young men who live in an entirely different world. It is a world where they are more accepted for their true selves without having to fit into a limited role applied to them by society. It is a world where a ten-year-old can discuss his sexuality by asking, "Meme, I don't know if I like boys or girls." I happily said, "Honey, you don't have to know that right now. You have plenty of time to make that decision. When it is time, it will become apparent to you."

I am so happy and proud of our country and how much we have changed in the last fifty years. I am not so happy about what has happened to marriages and families. Good examples of what a marriage commitment is and what it takes to have a good marriage are rare, so our divorce rates are still too high. According to the American Psychological Association, divorce rates for first marriages are 40 to 50 percent and 60 to 70 percent for second marriages.[1] However, this is a downward trend since 1990. That's a little bit of encouragement.

---

[1] Qtd. in "Divorce Statistics for 2022," Petrelli Previtera, accessed January 17, 2024, https://www.petrellilaw.com/divorce-statistics-for-2022/#:~:text=U.S.%202022%20Divorce%20Statistics%2C%20compiled,second%20marriages%20end%20in%20divorce.

This discussion is about choosing the right man and meeting my third husband. Yes, my twenties were a crazy and busy time. My original theory of love conquers all did not work. I had somehow, without knowing it after two failed marriages, come up with a vision of what I didn't want and would not settle for. I listed any of the behaviors that had not worked for me in my prior relationships. I was only partially right in this process. Knowing what you don't want is part of the equation. Even better is knowing what you want, and having a written description is even better.

It is so easy to be dating, meet a man who you are attracted to, and think he is the one. You are physically attracted to him and decide to have sex. However, he has a couple of beliefs that are different from yours or behaviors that you question. You tell yourself he will change, or you can make him change for you. Pay attention ladies. You cannot change a person into the person you want. He or she needs to be the person you are looking for. Do not settle for less, because it will come back to bite you in the ass. Sexual attraction cannot be the reason to get into a relationship. Yes, it is very important to a relationship, but it cannot be the only connection for a long-term relationship. If that is all you want, fine, have fun, but if you want more than that, don't pursue it. You will be hurt. There is nothing wrong with recreational safe sex unless you are going against your religious beliefs or the standards you have set for yourself. If you have sex with someone to please that person and you are going against your personal standards, you are hurting yourself. This could be a chapter. You must have more interests and similarities for a long-term relationship, not just a sexual connection.

I want you to write down some of the characteristics and values you know you would want in a man you would consider marrying. When I met Mike in 1980, I had a list of traits I would not have in my life. I didn't have the awareness to write down what I wanted or what my two children wanted or deserved. I don't want you to find your true mate by making bad choices. Have a clear vision in your mind all the time you are dating and on paper for you to remind yourself.

When I finally wrote my list, it was fairly short and limited to the important things. It was not a list of things that would always be there no matter who you had in your life: picks up his clothes, has blue eyes like Paul Newman, or puts the toothpaste cover on all the way, and so on.

Mine is someone who:

- Believes in God or is spiritual.
- Can provide for himself.
- Loves his family.
- Volunteers or gives of himself/is a generous person with time and money.
- Is kind and loving and not afraid to show it.
- Is not addicted to anything.
- Loves life and people, and is adventurous; and
- Dances and loves music, but this is not a deal breaker.

When you're dating, you will want to keep this in mind. Yes, a marriage can work if the other person doesn't want to go to church, but how great would it be if he or she went with you and shared those experiences? If the other cannot provide for himself or herself, it is not acceptable. If he or she doesn't want children, it will not work if you do, or you already have them. What is on your list should not be compromised ever. If you're out with someone and the person says he or she does not want children, don't move the relationship forward. Have a nice evening and know that person is not the right one—period, the end, goodbye, so long. There is no need to continue. Seriously, it is a waste of time for both of you. *Do not compromise!*

This list is your future. Most importantly, you deserve to have your best mate. Do not settle; be patient and know you will have what you deserve. Envision and keep that person on your list in your heart. Believe the universe will provide you with the person meant for you, so just be patient.

A woman, if she wants children, would want to have it on her list. No matter where you are in your life, the requirements represent what you need or desire in a man.

What are your requirements for your lifetime mate?

_____

_____

_____

_____

_____

_____

_____

_____

_____

_____

_____

_____

_____

_____

Dating and Red Flags

RITING THIS SECTION IS DIFFICULT FOR ME BECAUSE I TEND TO BELIEVE THE best in others. I walk around thinking that everyone is a good person and has everyone's best interests at heart. Unfortunately, that is not true. Others have had life experiences that have left them unable to understand what love is and how to behave lovingly in the world. This is not a cultural conversation but a spiritual one. This conversation is directed at dating and choosing a mate.

This section focuses on women dating but it could apply to men as well. We often attract people of the same vibration as like draws like, so if you are in a low vibration, you are more likely to draw someone of the same vibration. If you have high self-esteem and are living a high vibration, you will draw people to you of the same vibration. It is very important to do the work on yourself and love yourself, so you attract people of the same level of self-esteem. Empathic people of high vibration are targets for wounded souls who are looking for people to pull them out of their low vibration. Be aware of the signs of people who do not have the best of intentions and are in a relationship with you because of what you can give them. This is very important to know or to remember you cannot heal another person.

In the ten years since my husband passed, I attempted to date online, and I went on six different dates over a period of two or three years. I found it a very slow process, and a lot of work with few rewards. The lunch dates I went on were all varied and resulted in no second dates. I encountered more scammers than potential dates. I have seen a handful of couples who have had great relationships, even long-distance ones. I won't even begin to make a judgment on how it works. Who knows? Maybe I'll try it out again and see what happens but with a different attitude. However, I have learned in my lifetime some red flags to watch out for.

Red Flags

1. Gaslighting is the act or practice of grossly misleading someone, especially for one's own advantage. Examples would be questioning your intelligence, saying you said things you didn't, and so on.

2. Ghosting is the act or practice of abruptly cutting off all contact with someone (such as a former romantic partner), usually without explanation, by no longer accepting or responding to phone calls, instant messages, and so on.

3. Breadcrumbing involves barely giving you enough attention to keep you interested so you won't date or become interested in someone else.

4. The person lacks interest in you and doesn't want to hear anything about your personal life. This person talks only about himself or herself and is irritated when you switch the conversation to yourself.

5. The person lacks empathy for you or others.

6. An arrogant person will put you or others down for no reason except to make himself or herself feel superior.

7. The person loses his or her temper easily.

8. The person has unrealistic expectations of you and attempts to control you. The person may see you as his or her possession. This person can become jealous, controlling, demanding, and manipulative.

9. The person plays the victim to gain sympathy and attention from others.

10. The person always looks at other people or tries to make you jealous.

11. The person does not have money to take you out but finds money to go out with his or her friends.

12. The person gossips about others, puts others down, and talks negatively in general.

13. The person has emotional highs and lows.

14. The person gambles, drinks, takes drugs, or exhibits other excessive behavior.

15. The person does not make you a priority and is not there when you need him or her.

Most of all, trust your gut. Don't rush into a relationship before you know you can trust the other person. Most everyone wants to please you when you are first dating. Some men and women only want to get into their partners' pants. If you want to have sex, then have it. Recreational sex can be fun, but if you want to find the right partner, you can't let sexual passion get in your way. It will muddy the water and confuse the relationship. You find out who a person really is by spending time with the person, getting to know him or her, and learning about his or her world. If you hold off on sex, a person only looking for sex will not continue much beyond the third date. If the person is still around after three dates, then he or she cares for you and wants to get to know you. Don't spoil the best time in your dating process by rushing through it. Courting is an exciting and passionate time in building the foundation of trust and communicating who you are and what your dreams are. You will know when the right time is. You will feel it in your heart and your soul.

Most caring people and empaths want to help those who are hurt and wounded; however, all healing has to be done by them. No matter how much we want to do it for them, it is their responsibility. They must work on their own baggage, so stop trying to carry it for them. Then, you will have more time to work on being even more beautiful yourself.

Have you ever encountered a mate who had any of the qualities above? What lesson did you learn?

_____

_____

_____

_____

_____

_____

_____

_____

_____

_____

_____

_____

_____

_____

What will you do in the future to ensure you attract the right person and follow your plan?

_____

_____

_____

_____

_____

_____

_____

_____

_____

_____

_____

_____

_____

Being Responsible

THE HAPPIEST TIMES IN MY LIFE ARE WHEN I AM IN A RELATIONSHIP WITH another human being. While I do appreciate solitary and peaceful moments, I experience most of my happiness and joy with my heart connected to another. Most people who were not around me as a child would argue that I am far from shy. As children, we were discouraged from speaking when we were out in public. The old directive "children should be seen and not heard" applied. If we misbehaved and had to be spoken to, we paid a price when we got home. Consequently, I never learned to express myself and feel confident until I was over thirty. I went to college and began years of groups around addictions, spiritual growth, and healing therapy with polarity and reiki. I am sure people will tell you I am a leader and speak up with firm honesty. I have been told sometimes I can be too honest.

We have already discussed being in relationships with men, telling the truth in a relationship, what we want for long-term relationships and our relationship with ourselves and other women. We don't have enough time to discuss our relationships with our mothers or fathers other than they are the most important relationships of our lives, in my opinion. The love we receive or do not receive, the lessons they teach us or don't teach us will affect how we respond to people for the rest of our lives. How much we accept them or don't is a direct reflection of how much we accept ourselves. They are our parents, and we had no choice in who we got. Some people would argue that, if you believe in reincarnation, you can choose them when you return.

We discussed forgiveness and acceptance. Now, I would like to discuss responsibility for your own happiness. When I was a child, my parents were always seeking out which one of us committed the crime. I learned a very valuable lesson to fess up and take responsibility for whatever we did. That lesson has followed me through my life, sometimes easily and sometimes not so easily. However, I believe the biggest responsibility is being responsible for your own happiness.

Do not expect someone else to bring you happiness and don't wait for it to come to you. You will find the only way to have happiness is to believe in yourself and manifest what you want in your life. Don't be a victim of your own behaviors and thoughts. If your relationships are not what you want them to be, act. If you aren't having the relationship you want, find the courage and trust yourself to approach your friend, your child, or your spouse and work it out. If you want something, go get it. What is the worst that can happen? Certainly, it could be no worse than sitting back and expecting someone else to guess what you want and bring you happiness. You are setting them up to fail and you continue to be a victim. If your siblings or your grandchildren haven't called, pick up the phone and call them. Don't sit back and make them wrong because they haven't reached out. If you're not happy with your job, change it. If your marriage isn't what you want it to be, please work together on it. Love yourself enough to take the chance to have everything you want. If it does not happen the way you wanted, at least you know why and can do something else that reaps the rewards you want. Love yourself enough to get what you want and take the risk. Do not settle. You deserve to have your dreams.

What are your next steps? What risks do you need to take to make yourself happier?

_____

_____

_____

_____

_____

_____

_____

_____

_____

_____

_____

_____

_____

What stops you from making the changes necessary?

_____

_____

_____

_____

_____

_____

_____

_____

_____

_____

_____

_____

_____

_____

Speaking the Truth

I HAVE BEEN FACED WITH NOT WANTING TO CONFRONT SOMEONE WITH A DIFFICULT situation and been concerned about injuring or offending him or her. What is the appropriate way to approach the person? I feel we can say anything to anyone if we say it in the right way. If we speak from our hearts and with a good attitude, the most uncomfortable situations and problems can have positive results.

We are always learning what we need, whether we want to or not. The universe gave me what I needed to learn with 500 to 600 men. I received plenty of practice. Many of my careers have put me in positions of conflict and of being the bearer of bad news or disappointment to others. I learned many lessons when I worked as a health, welfare, and pension representative to our local pipefitters' union and electricians' union. I had overcome some of my fears of men by that time and was about to learn more on how to deal with angry men.

Being the bearer of bad news seemed a daily occurrence. The most important useful tool for me was to remember that their anger was driven by their fear. These fears included not having the money to pay for health insurance when they or their family members were sick. They also feared not being able to obtain any pension funds to help them keep their homes. I was the keeper of the rules and had to bear the bad news. This was no time for my ego to come out to protect me. This was when I would reach into my heart and be with them where they were. I would have the conversation as someone who cared for them and would help them in any way I could. When they felt my compassion and knew I was there for them, doing my best to help them, and was not the enemy, we could then begin the work of finding solutions. Sometimes there were none, but they left knowing they had a friend, and they were understood and not alone. I learned not to have a relationship with their attitudes (ego) but with the people beneath.

How do I support my best friend or family member when I don't want to tell the person the truth for fear he or she will become unhappy or angry? So many times, I have been confronted with telling someone the truth when it would be so much easier to just forget about it. Maybe the person did not want to hear it or maybe I wanted to please the person. Maybe someone has asked you to talk about something that is important and may affect his or her entire life. The person may have a big decision to make, and asks for your opinion. Do not speak from your ego and think you know what is best for him or her. You must throw that idea right out of the equation, speak from love and compassion, and tell the person the truth.

Recently, a friend of mine divorced. She was upset that we hadn't told her how unhealthy her husband and her marriage were. She thought we should have told her to leave him. I reminded her that she knew who and what he was, but she had asked us to support her in staying and being a good wife and mother. Her children are all grown, and now we are supporting her through this process because it is what she wants. We can tell others our thoughts and feelings but, in the end, it is always their choice. Be honest with your friend, co-worker, or family member so he or she can make the right choices for himself or herself. Never recommend what the person should or should not do. Don't let your ego's attitude convince you that you know what is best for that person. You don't. Only the other person does. Provide him or her with a loving, judgement-free space where he or she can feel safe and there is plenty of time to *just be*. Ask the person the questions you know he or she needs to hear so the person can find his or her own answers.

The person has the answers inside but does not know how to express them. The person may believe others will judge him or her, or even that he or she is unworthy. The person knows his or her truth.

Don't be afraid to say what you see and express how you feel. If you're angry with another person about something, think it through first. Come from a place where you want to tell the person how it felt to you and not what he or she did to hurt you. Speak about what you felt, not what the other person did. Remember, that person is your friend and never intended to hurt you. If the person did, he or she is not your friend. Friends don't hurt friends intentionally.

How do you feel when you have to address someone who is angry and what would you like to tell him or her?

_____

_____

_____

_____

_____

_____

_____

_____

_____

_____

_____

_____

_____

Is there someone from whom you are withholding the truth or your feelings?

_____

_____

_____

_____

_____

_____

_____

_____

_____

_____

_____

_____

_____

Awareness-Forgiveness-Acceptance

WHAT CAUSES SOMEONE TO ASK FOR FORGIVENESS? DOES THE PERSON NEED to forgive himself or herself or someone else? When I think of this question, I think of the harm my actions or someone else's actions caused, the pain, sadness, regrets, and unsaid words. Why would anyone want to bring up all those feelings again or discuss what happened to cause them? Immediately, I go to how I can fix it or what my responsibility is. I process and analyze it for whatever amount of time it takes for me to come to an understanding. Ultimately, I come to some peace. This can come immediately or take months. I know that it is beneficial to work through whatever I need to for me to move on and find forgiveness for myself or others. If I don't, the weight will be a burden that I do not want to carry. The pain also continues or worsens. Not only does it influence how I feel about myself or anyone involved, but it can carry over to other relationships as well. The feelings that I associate with unforgiveness are sadness, anger, disrespect, shame, and loneliness. When I analyzed the process, I found three distinct levels necessary for me to be forgiving: awareness, acceptance, and forgiveness.

Awareness: Usually, it is easy to know when you have been hurt because you feel it. Realizing you have harmed someone else is not as easy unless the person tells you; then, it is apparent. Admitting to myself that I may have caused harm to someone else is never easy. I realize I am human and make mistakes. Sometimes, in my own pain, I just don't care enough to notice, my awareness is very limited. I'm in the "me" world and my ego is protecting me by shutting off all awareness that I caused myself or someone else sadness. Not everyone you harm is fearless enough to express that you have harmed them.

Acceptance: At some point of self-reflection, I take responsibility and own up to what I am responsible for. I realize the harm that someone else has or I have done that I need to forgive. I think it is easier to forgive others when they are asking for forgiveness but much harder when they don't ask. They may not even want it or realize they have done anything to harm you. Perhaps they are in the ego space where they don't care or are unable to ask for it. Whether they are aware or not, you still must decide if you are going to tell them or just forgive them in your heart because you both need it. When I have done something that has caused me pain, it is usually followed by being pissed off at myself for my bad decisions. I question my sanity and then realize I am only "human." I seek out the lesson to be learned and forgive myself. I know that everything that happens in life has a lesson. I must be a genius by now.

Forgiveness: Forgiving myself is easier than asking for forgiveness from others because I feel more shame for what I have done that caused them harm. When I ask for forgiveness, I am required to be humble, fearless, and vulnerable, welcoming and receiving all that the other person feels and needs to say. They may not be able to forgive me at that moment or understand why I did what I did. I may have to wait for forgiveness from them and be prepared that maybe he or she won't forgive me. However, I know I have done everything I can. In conclusion, I forgive myself and move on knowing I have done my best.

Is there something you need to take responsibility for? Do you need to forgive yourself for causing harm? What is the lesson you can learn?

_____

_____

_____

_____

_____

_____

_____

_____

_____

_____

_____

_____

_____

_____

What do you need to accept and forgive someone else for?

_____

_____

_____

_____

_____

_____

_____

_____

_____

_____

_____

_____

_____

_____

_____

Spirituality

*I*KNOW SO LITTLE ABOUT THIS SUBJECT. MOST WOULD SAY I PROBABLY SHOULD NOT be writing about it. However, I am because I have experienced numerous events. Even more than that, I am aware of how my soul is feeling and how it affects me and those around me. This will be a discussion of my own experiences, thoughts, and feelings about spirit and soul. Throughout my life, I have had experiences of seeing auras, sensing sudden messages, being urged to do things unexpectedly, and seeing things happen in dreams before they did in reality.

As a child and a few times as an adult, I have been able to see a person's aura, a field of soft light surrounding the outline of the body. I couldn't see it with everybody or at any time, and it only happened with women. I could see my teacher's energy field around her body in the classroom. The atmosphere was quiet, and the sun was shining brightly into the room. Her energy was vibrant and soft white. The only other times I was able to see auras were of two classmates in polarity school. The atmosphere was pure, the air was clean, and we meditated and cleared our chakras.

I dreamed of my brother's unforeseen car accident the night before it happened. I witnessed my mother-in-law Francis speak to her deceased husband the night of her death. I was summoned energetically to my mother-in-law Laura's deathbed. I sensed or knew that I needed to be there. Another time, I was sitting at home at 10:30 at night with a girlfriend and was unexpectedly summoned to the bedside of a man. We found the friend's pillow smoldering fire, and we saved his life. While I had a close connection with this person, I would not have been going to his home at that time of night. It was quite alarming that I had such a need to go without knowing why. I witnessed my husband speaking to his brother the night before he passed. This told me he would not be here much longer.

There was a period in the 90s when I was more connected to myself physically, emotionally, and spiritually. I had done a lot of work on my relationships with myself and with others. I learned to express my feelings and began my process of healing and healing others. My forties were the beginning of my spiritual connection on a different level. My children had left the house, and I was left with all this time to focus on myself for the first time in my life. I was open to finding out how to be responsible for my own happiness.

The universe sent me in two different directions. One was to heal my soul by surrounding myself with women to teach me about self-acceptance and love for myself and others. The other was physical healing through polarity therapy when I decided to become a polarity therapist. Both avenues were of giving and receiving all that needed to move myself into a spiritual connection with others. I am so grateful for what I learned. My personal growth brought me to an amazing time in my life. I want to encourage you to notice the messages you are being sent from spirit, God, universal energy, higher power, or whatever you believe in. For those of you who choose to believe in nothing, notice what your intuition is telling you. Notice what you feel in your gut. We are continuously receiving messages from the soul, heart, and gut telling us when something is not right or is perfect. We just need to be in tune.

Have you ever been doing something and heard yourself say, "You might want to do something another way" or "You forgot something"? Maybe you ignored it and moved on only to find out that the message was correct, and it would have been wise to have listened. Maybe you thought about an old friend you had not seen in years, and then the person called, or you bumped into the person. Maybe you thought of a friend you haven't seen or talked to and found out he or she passed away the same day as your thought. We, and everyone and everything around us is energy. Energy draws like energy; negativity draws negativity and positivity draws positivity. Be careful what you are thinking about the messages that come from nowhere. I continuously check my thoughts to see if they are in line with how I want to live my life. I am aware of messages that are being sent to me by a higher spirit. It's a bit like a child who you are trying to toilet train who does not care; you end up having to clean up some messes.

The most important thing I have learned in being able to recognize I am receiving or open to receiving messages is my physical and mental health. I cannot even begin to see, feel, and recognize anything spiritual if I am not well and aligned physically. If my energy fields are not open, especially my third eye and frontal lobe, the ability to see or feel energy is blocked. If it is blocked, there is no communication or ability for me to see my connection. When it is open, there is a circle of glowing light in the middle of my forehead that changes in size and color depending on the level of connection to spirit. When I am in perfect alignment or something wonderful has happened, it is purple or violet. Normally, it is white, and the few times it's been black, these were times I have been very sick.

Here are some of the ways I keep myself in alignment.

- Breathing sounds like a simple thing, but notice that, when you are angry or frightened, your breathing is faster and shallow. When you begin to feel the stress in your neck, head, or other parts of your body, take deep, slow breaths in your nose and exhale slow long breaths out of your mouth. It's very difficult to be aware of the messages your body is sending when everything is blocked. Energy will move in your body until it reaches the next block, so pay attention to those areas that hurt or are stiff. You can find much information on YouTube on breathing as well as CDs for chakra clearings that are wonderful.

- Mediating: I always thought I wasn't benefitting from meditation because I would fall asleep or could not keep my mind from thinking. I was waiting for the quiet space with no conversation. What I found was that even if I only rested my eyes for a few minutes, I would wake feeling renewed. If I went into my meditation with questions for spirit, there would be answers. When you clear your mind and it is silent, you will hear your messages, sometimes referred to as "downloads."

- Rest is so important for maintaining good alignment and clear thinking. If you are tired and can't think straight, it is nearly impossible to receive the messages. Most of my communication with the spirit world is in the middle of the night when it is peaceful. I believe the angels find it easier to communicate then.

- Eat healthily: I don't believe in dieting. However, eating a healthy and balanced diet and drinking alcohol only in moderation are good practices. This is very enjoyable for me, and I love to cook. When you are taking care of yourself and giving your body what it needs, the connection to source is much stronger.

- Fun and laughter are mandatory for having a healthy, good spirit and open heart.

- Music lifts a person's spirit and resonates with every cell in the body. We can be reminded of pleasant memories. We hear and feel the sound creating passionate and peaceful feelings within us. Sound is an incredible healer, whether you are toning, listening to crystal bowls, drumming, or using tuning forks. They can clear the mind, body, and soul. When I have been meditating and I feel completely connected, toning happens naturally for me.

- Creativity: When I can tap into being creative, it brings joy. Joy comes from the process not the expectations. Creating is the part of me that is unafraid to show my imagination. When I have kept judgment out of my head, not been stuck on directions or what others were doing, and allowed my spirit to guide me, I created the butterflies in the book as a representation of change, beauty and freedom.

- Try reiki, polarity, or any therapy that will open energy fields and help you relax or overcome anxiety. This improved the flow of energy through my body and keeps my chakras clear.

- Motion is important not just to strengthen our body but to keep our chakras open. My favorite is dancing which I try to do at least once a week.

Notice there is no mention of exercise programs and that is because I have none. I do love to dance, and I figure that is a wonderful way to stay fit. I dance a lot in the kitchen. A little Jimi Hendrix gets me going in the morning and makes me smile. Have you ever frowned while you're dancing? It just doesn't seem right. I don't know what's out there, but I know too many situations that have caused me to believe. I'm going to keep asking for help and listening to the spirit and all its helpers for downloads or messages.

When no one is looking, who are you listening to?

Are there any experiences you cannot explain? Do you feel someone intervened in those experiences?

_____

_____

_____

_____

_____

_____

_____

_____

_____

_____

_____

_____

_____

Affirmations / Compliments

IN MY CHILDHOOD HOME, WE DID NOT HEAR COMPLIMENTS OR GIVE THEM. WE heard "love you" every night when we went to bed, but we never received compliments from our parents. If we did, I do not recall them. We also did not know what it meant to set goals for our future. Females in the late 1960s at my economic level were destined to get married and have babies, and I followed the plan.

I have already mentioned affirmations were part of my self-improvement and personal growth during the 1980s. I am a firm believer that affirmations and positive reinforcement do inspire us and change our belief in ourselves. This is true whether we created our own or someone else has written ones that connect to us and inspire us.

Before I started this conversation, I was resting my eyes. Okay, I fell asleep, and the word *compliment* was part of my thoughts around affirmations. I wondered what the difference between a compliment and an affirmation was, so I decided to look them up. I really was not excited about the definition of affirmation as a declaration of the truth of something. How had I come to love my affirmations and be inspired by them so much? This is a declaration of the truth of myself. My favorite affirmation that dressed up my bathroom mirror for years was "I grow better and better every day in every way." I read that over and over every day, and it did become the truth for me. It also was a compliment. A compliment is an expression of pride, commendation, or admiration. I was complimenting myself because I was getting better and better in every way. My growth during that time was endless and is continuing. You are never too old to learn more about yourself and others to say nothing of technology. I'm still learning how to edit a Word document. It feels good to compliment yourself or others.

I was working as a volunteer for our local theater at an outside concert and was passing out free drawing tickets for a drawing at the end. I passed a handsome younger man who decided to buy a 50/50 ticket also and he said, "You look beautiful in that dress." That took me back for a moment. I thanked him for the compliment and wondered if the woman next to him was his sister. I thought about asking but changed my mind as it probably wouldn't have been appropriate. I am still appreciating the unexpected compliment. I feel a bit embarrassed by them because I don't receive them often. Usually, women unexpectedly say I'm beautiful. I feel that is because at that moment, I reflect how they feel about themselves and life, which is loving and generous. They are of the same spirit and open to feeling and seeing other people's energy. For example, let's say I'm seated in a restaurant. I see a woman and I feel the love oozing from her. Her energy is so beautiful. As she leaves, she stops at our table to say, "I just have to say you are so beautiful." Those moments are all around us when we see inner beauty flowing out into the universe. We need to acknowledge it and I feel grateful for those moments when we take time to see it in others.

My affirmation now is "trust the universe" There are so many uncertainties as I age, and I am alone. I just get up and start each day trusting the universe. I can get myself in a pickle with all the questions racing in my head without satisfying answers. I continue to remind myself I do not have to have the answers. I need to trust that the universe will take care of the questions I need answers to. If I am clear about what I want to happen, move my thoughts to where I want to be in my state of being, happy, peaceful, and safe, and feel as if I already have the answer, then the universe moves everything I want to me. Like draws like.

Whatever you want or need to have (a new romance, a new home, or a new job), create a clear vision of it. Even if you don't know how you are going to get it, create an affirmation around it or a vision board. Let your affirmation be what is true for you even if it does not seem possible. Trust it is going to happen, and act like it has. For example, I could post an affirmation that I am healthier every day. Then, I could write what needs to be done: lose weight, quit smoking, quit an addiction, start running, act healthy, begin eating healthily, and exercise like I am healthy. Obviously, you are not going out to do 100 sit-ups or five-mile runs, but a walk around the block would be a good start.

Affirmations and compliments are my expressions of truth and admiration, showing love and acceptance in all I do. I know you think that is easy for me because I'm old and I have had lots of experience. However, it is my experience that sometimes you forget what you learned and must relearn it, especially if you learned it forty years ago. Second, I've become short-tempered and forget I said I was going to *be* loving. Third, I have just learned to speak up for myself and I might like being able to be a little combative. The bottom line is it isn't easy being loving all the time, but it is worth the shot. Most of all, living consciously about others is the most important tool in my toolbox. When writing my affirmations I find it is better if I write it in the present tense, such as "I am health and active", I am love.

For years, I had many affirmations and visions for my life in my bathroom mirror. Here are a few of them.

- I am better and better every day, in every way.
- I am a beautiful soul.
- I am perfect just the way I am.
- I trust the universe.
- I will love and respect my own needs.
- I will live in love.

On the final page of your journal is a page of beautifully blocked-off sections to write a few truths and admirations for yourself. I have taken one space to write what I would like. You can place it on your mirror if you choose.

What are your expressions of truth and admiration for yourself?

_____

_____

_____

_____

_____

_____

_____

_____

_____

_____

_____

_____

_____

_____

What are your goals/visions for your future?

_____

_____

_____

_____

_____

_____

_____

_____

_____

_____

_____

_____

_____

Closure

My mom passed away before I was able to complete this journal. I was in the final editing when she left this earth. She had a vision of a staircase. I thought she was telling me to "wash the stairs." She said, "No, watch the stairs." I asked her if she saw someone and she said, "Yes, Mama." How wonderful if the person to meet her was her mama, who she hadn't seen since she was two and a half. It made my heart sing. I'm sure my brother was there as well.

There are women in my life who I love and respect, who have contributed to my success as a woman. They and so many other women have taught me so much about myself as they are my reflection. I strongly suggest you surround yourself with people you admire. They may have what you want in your life or live how you want to live. They may have learned the lessons you need to learn. Make them your mentors. They will become your extended family by choice.

This book can be completed by you in your own time, in your own way. It can also be beneficial to do with other people as a book study, or with a friend you trust and who knows you well. There are many benefits of an intimate conversation and revealing yourself to a non-judgmental friend who will share his or her experiences with you and what he or she sees in you with honest, healthy expressions. This is how true intimacy is formed and love is received and given. I hope when you look in your mirror and you read your affirmations each morning you are saying "Hello Beautiful". So I happily leave you with "Hello beautiful."

Bibliography

"Divorce Statistics for 2022." Petrelli Previtera. Accessed January 17, 2024. https://www. petrellilaw.com/divorce-statistics-for-2022/#:~:text=U.S.%202022%20Divorce%20 Statistics%2C%20compiled,second%20marriages%20end%20in%20divorce.

Hello beautiful
You are right where
you are supposed to be.
Trust in the process and
yourself. Find your joy.

Printed in the United States
by Baker & Taylor Publisher Services